GROW CBD INDOORS

Author: Jay P. Surfe
Publisher: CBD Reviews LLC

ISBN: 9781687005489

For permissions contact: media@cbd.how

DEDICATION

My heart goes out to the loves of my life A.N. and B.R. Without your continued love, guidance, and support none of this would be possible and I am forever grateful.

CONTENTS

ACKNOWLEDGEMENTS

Thank you D.K./ E.A. / T.M. for going on this grow journey together and sharing wisdom with each other along the way.

Thank you Bevon and Melissa from CBD REVIEWS for supporting my dreams and giving me a platform to work together to bring accurate and transparent CBD information to the masses.

Bio: This DIY hemp grow guide is targeted towards anyone who wants to better their life by growing their own CBD medicine. We have put together a simple guide on how to grow your own CBD enriched hemp plants indoors. Our goal is to educate the public on this life saving and environmentally friendly process.

Hello there, my name is Jay P. Surfe. I have chronic back pain, anxiety, arthritis, and Crohn's disease. After working with Bevon and CBD Reviews, I found that CBD was able to drastically reduce all my ailments.

I immediately began growing my own CBD hoping to make my own medicine. There have multiple ups and downs, planting, re-planting, and everything in between.

I hope to save the CBD community time and money by providing readers with information necessary to prevent my mistakes from happening to them.

SUPPLIES LIST

This is the exact list of items used in this book and the pictures associated with it:

- LED Light (*prefer LED because it is cheaper on electric bill and lower on heat*)
- 3x3x6 feet tent
- Happy Frog Soil
- CBD seeds
- 3-gallon pots
- Pot trays to fit 3-gallon cloth pots
- Solo Cup
- Clear plastic cup
- Ionic Nutrient Kit (Plant Food)
- Circulating Fan for inside tent (if you are worried about smell intake fan and carbon filter (this is not necessary if smell is not an issue)
- Pullies for light
- Timer for light
- Temp and humidity gauge
- Spray bottle
- Automatic timer
- Power strip
- Extension cord
- Trimming scissors
- Tweezers
- Empty Mason Jars

TENT SETUP

Find a spot that will fit your grow tent and is close to a power outlet. Follow the instructions that came with your tent to set it up properly.

Once the tent is put together, set up your power strip close to the tent so all things can be plugged in accurately. Put circulating fan on ground.

Put your temp and humidity gauge on the floor of the tent or can hang it in the tent. Place empty pot trays with the empty 3-gallon pots into the tent, (We do this to make sure you can visualize your grow space).

Use your pulleys to hang your LED grow light in the middle of the tent on the cross beams that came with your tent. Make sure to plug the grow light into the automatic timer on the power strip.

As neatly as possible take wires from light, inside circulating fan, and plug them in to the power strip.

BASICS OF YOUR GROW ENVIRONMENT

70-80 degrees with lights on, 60-70 when lights are off. Relative humidity for seedling stage 55-65%, relative humidity for grow stage 45-55%, relative humidity for flower stage 40-50%.

These humidity's don't have to be exact, but anything over 70% could cause mold and anything under 30% could harm your plants. Air needs to be flowing throughout the tent, with fresh air always coming in (circulating fan will help with both).

Just like in nature, you want your plants to have a slight air flow over them. This is important for all stages of a grow because it helps strengthen the main stalk of the plant, making it sturdy enough to handle the weight of the CBD flowers.

This also provides less chances of mold and bugs interfering with your grow environment.

I suggest leaving lights and fans on 24 hours before anything is planted, to see how the tent and your grow environment reacts to your new set up.

NUTRIENTS

Since our plant is being grown indoors under artificial UV lights, it is important to provide your plant with proper nutrients.

There are multiple companies with multiple step systems out there for feeding your plants.

For simplicity, we recommend using "IONIC" BRAND NUTRIENTS.

It is a simple three step system:

One for GROW, one for BLOOM, and a BOOST ENHANCER to improve the performance of the base nutrients and give mass to your CBD flowers.

PH

pH is a measure of how acidic/basic water is. This is important to check before each watering because the pH of water determines how your nutrients are dissolved into water and the plant's ability to ingest it.

Essentially, this is key to your plant sucking up the water carrying its food to it. This is easily obtainable on Amazon or at any indoor gardening store. With the pH kits, green is base and red is acidic.

It comes with a pH up bottle and a pH down bottle that will help you get the correct balance.

Read instructions with kit if you have any questions on how to use. Optimized nutrition intake occurs around 5.8% - 6.5%, which is color indicated on your test bottle.

It is usually a darkish yellow/green. Don't get frustrated if it takes you multiple attempts to get this correct.

GROW AND BLOOM

Basic Grow Stage Info

Since our plant is being grown indoors under artificial UV lights, it is important to provide your plant with proper nutrients.

There are multiple companies with multiple step systems out there for feeding your plants.

For simplicity, we recommend using "IONIC" BRAND NUTRIENTS.

It is a simple three step system:

Basic Bloom Stage Info

"Bloom" is the stage where your plant starts to produce the CBD flower. During the bloom phase your lights will be on for 12 hours and turned off for 12 hours.

We do this to simulate the sun's rise and fall during the colder months. This tricks the plant into thinking winter is near. Prior to this stage, your plant will appear only as leaves and stalks, so don't worry if it takes up to 3-4 weeks to show the first CBD flowers.

During those 3-4 weeks before flowers show, your plant will undergo "stretch".

Your plant could double in height during this stage before the CBD flower shows.

We suggest keeping your plants in the Bloom phase for 60-90 days. This time all depends on the strain, seed genetics, and grow environment.

Bloom

Seed Start

Let's start with the very beginning.

Grab a cup, fill it with distilled water (not cold and not hot. Luke-warm is best.) and drop a seed into it (the seed should float on the top). Leave it in a warm dark place. (ex by router back of a computer etc.) wait for your seed to sink to the bottom... or carefully inspect it for a crack.

This is helping the seed absorb water so it can start to "crack" the hard shell and start to grow a root. In as early as one day to as late as 7 days your seed should start to be showing a small white tail. Once your tail is as long as a fingernail, you are ready to put it into a rapid rooter.

WATERING SEEDLING AND FIRST FOUR WATERINGS

Starting Your Seedling

Start with a basic solo cup. On the bottom of that cup you need to make multiples holes about the size of a ballpoint pen tip. We do this so the solo cup can drain the water we are giving to our baby early on.

Fill the solo cup halfway with soil. Slightly give it a spray it with a spray bottle until soil is wet all the way on the top. Add the other half of soil to the cup and gently spray it down so it is moist.

Push two fingers into the soil in the middle of the cup until you reach halfway between your first knuckle and second knuckle. Make a circular motion with your

fingers until there is a hole big enough for the rapid rooter to go into.

Gently use a pair of tweezers and place your seed (tail facing down) into the hole in the rapid rooter and place a small amount of loose dirt inside the top of the hole. Place the rapid rooter in the hole you made in the soil and gently pack the soil in around it.

Lightly spray the dirt you have just packed around the rapid rooter until soil is moist.

DO NOT spray the rapid rooter itself. Place it under your light which should be about 28-36 inches away from your cup. Mist the inside of the clear cup with spray bottle and place it on top of your solo cup to keep humidity and moisture in. This is very important for the early stages of your seedling.

A minimum of 2 mists daily...once in the morning and once at night. You will also need to mist the soil around the rapid rooter itself every day same time you decide to mist the solo cup.

Usually seedlings take 1-7 days to sprout out of the soil. Once your seed starts to sprout and show leaves...this will be considered Day 1 for your plant. Once the leaves show, you will no longer use the clear cup to keep the moisture in.

You will still spray and mist the soil of the seedling for the next 1-2 weeks. Once the leaves of your seedling can reach the sides of the cups or even extend the sides then it's time to transfer.

You need to give your plant about 2-3 days of no misting before you transfer so the soil doesn't crumble on you.

Transplant from solo cup to growing medium. Take your empty 3-gallon cloth pot, put it on top of your pot tray and fill it a fourth of the way with soil... make sure to move the dirt so it is evenly distributed.

Pour the water evenly so it's enough to sink through the soil and let it settle for a min. This process doesn't have to be perfect....

**The reason we are doing this is for a later step when we begin to water. We don't want any air pockets in our soil from it seeping through unevenly.

Fill the pot with more soil enough to fill the pot ¾ of the way full. Repeat the water process to stop air pockets. Once you are certain the water has drained out the bottom, put an empty solo cup in the middle of the pot and fill rest of pot with soil so the empty cup has created a hole for the transfer of the seedling.

Grip the top of your seedling cup with your pointer finger and middle finger holding the seedling stem in between them. Gently flip your cup upside and wiggle out the soil by crunching the bottom of the cup and sides and letting gravity help the soil slide out.

Once you are holding the seedling and its dirt formed like the cup in your hand, flip it back over and place it in your previous hole we just made in the fresh cloth gallon pot.

TRANSPLANT

Fill in the rest of the opening with soil and smooth out the top of your new pot and seedling. Spray the top of the soil around the transfer hole with water.

You do not need to spray the plant we just transferred just everything around it.

Continue misting again for about two days. The fresh cloth pot should be placed on top of plant trays inside of tent. These are placed so all excess water can be drained out of cloth pot when it is being watered.

You do not want to leave your plants sitting in their own drained water, trays must be emptied 15 mins after watering.

WHEN AND HOW-TO WATER

Number one rule, there is no specific day count for when to water. All plants and all environments are different and could affect how much water the plant drinks, or how much water is evaporated. Touching and feeling are the only true ways to know when your plant is ready.

Lift your plant early on to get a feel of what it feels like dry. You will be able to tell if your plant needs watering based on how heavy or light it feels. Secondly, you can stick your pointer finger into the soil knuckle deep. If it is slightly moist there is probably no need to water, if dirt is dry and gritty it is time to water.

In my experience the larger the plant gets the faster it drinks the water. Remember it is normal for excess water to form in our pot trays. When this happens simply pour out the excess water and put plant back on the tray.

Lights are on a timer for 18 hours on 6 hours off

(Example: Lights off at 2:00 am and turn back on at 8:00 am)

How to Water Your Seedling: (Day 1-10)

From the day that your seed turns into a seedling, it is going to need water. For the early stages of the seedling we will need a large spray bottle and distilled water. Fill the spray bottle up with distilled water.

Each day you will mist the soil surrounding the rapid rooter, DO NOT spray rapid rooter the seed was original planted in. It does not need to be drenched, just enough to make the soil darker. I do this once in the morning and once at night.

Too much water early on can damage the fragile roots from your seedling.

First Grow Watering: (Day 10-12)

Lift your cloth planter to get a feel of what the plant feels like dry before watering. For the first watering we will use 2.5 cups of nutrient rich water. Measure out 2.5 cups of water, then add .5 teaspoon of the Ionic Grow nutrients.

Use your pH kit to check the nutrient enriched water to make sure the test shows a 5.8% to 6.5%. Once your water is pH'd properly we will spray the dirt with our distilled water to get the soil not dry.

Slowly and equally pour the water surrounding the rapid rooter in a circular motion. Pour about half the water, pause to let it soak into the soil, then finish pouring the rest of the water in a circular motion around the rapid rooter.

"Day 12"

Second Grow Seedling Watering: (Day 15-18)

The second watering will usually be 2-3 days after the first watering. All plants and conditions are different so no one plant will be the same. For the second watering we will be using 5 cups of water. Follow the exact same steps of the first watering, but you will not be adding nutrients.

Third Grow Watering: (Day 21-24)

The third watering will usually be 2-3 days after the second watering. For the third watering we will give our plant 8 cups of water. We will add 1 teaspoon of Ionic grow nutrients. After adding nutrients, we will need to PH the water.

Once water is pH'd we skip the water bottle spraying of the soil and will continue to water around the base of rapid rooter. It is normal with this amount of water for the water to start migrating to the edge of soil and the pot.

"Day 21"

Fourth Grow Watering: (Day 27-29)

The fourth watering will be about 3-4 days after the third watering. We will be watering our plant with ¾ of a gallon of water. The water will need to be pH'd. Once water is pH'd slowly and evenly distribute the water to the soil. Remember to stop halfway to let your plant drink the water, then pour rest of pH'd water into soil.

REST OF THE VEG CYCLE FEEDING

Day 30-33:

¾ gallon of water, 3 teaspoons ionic grow nutrients, pH'd.

Day 34-37:

¾ gallon of water, pH'd

"Day 34"

Day 40-43:

¾ gallon of water, 3 teaspoons Ionic grow nutrients, pH'd

Day 46-49:

¾ gallon of water, pH'd

Day 52-55:

1 gallon of water, 4 teaspoons Ionic grow nutrients, pH'd

Day 58-60:

¾ gallon of water, pH'd

"Day 60"

START OF BLOOM CYCLE

Lights are on a timer for 12 hours on 12 hours off

(Example lights off at 10:00pm and turn back on at 10:00am)

First Bloom Watering: (Day 60-63)

For the first bloom watering, we will use ¾ a gallon of nutrient rich water. Measure out ¾ gallon of water, then add 3 teaspoons of the Ionic Bloom nutrients and ¾ a teaspoon PK boost.

Use your pH kit to check the nutrient enriched water to make sure the test shows a pH of 5.8% to 6.5%. Slowly and equally pour the water surrounding the rapid rooter in a circular motion.

Pour about half the water, pause to let it soak into the soil, then finish pouring the rest of the water in a circular motion around the rapid rooter.

Second Bloom Watering: (Day 64-67)

The second watering will usually be 2-3 days after the first watering. All plants and conditions are different so no one plant will be the same.

For the second bloom watering we will be using ¾ gallon pH'd water. Follow the exact same steps of the first bloom watering, but you will not be adding nutrients.

Third Bloom Watering: (Day 70-73)

The third watering will usually be 2-3 days after the second watering. For the third watering we will give our plant ¾ gallon. We will add 3 teaspoons of Ionic bloom nutrients and ¾ teaspoon PK boost.

After adding nutrients, we will need to pH the water. Once water is pH'd we will continue to water around the base of rapid rooter. It is normal with this amount of water for the water to start migrated to the edge of soil and the pot.

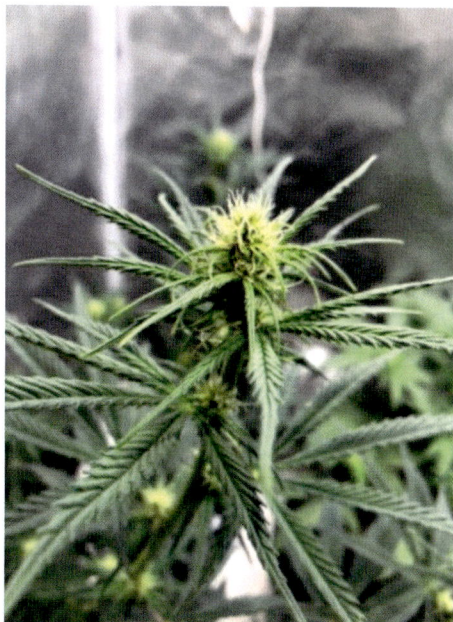

"Bloom Day 70"

Fourth Bloom Watering: (Day 74-77)

The fourth watering will be about 3-4 days after the third watering. We will be watering our plant with a ¾ of a gallon of water. The water will need to be pH'd.

Once water is pH'd slowly and evenly distribute the water to the soil. Remember to stop halfway to let your plant drink the water, then pour rest of pH'd water into soil.

"Bloom Day 74"

REST OF THE BLOOM CYCLE FEEDING

Day 80-83:

Gallon of water, 4 teaspoons ionic Bloom nutrients, 1.5 teaspoons PK boost, pH'd.

Day 84-87:

Gallon of water, pH'd

Day 90-93:

Gallon of water, 4 teaspoons Ionic Bloom nutrients, 1.5 teaspoons PK boost, pH'd

Day 96-99:

Gallon of water, 1.5 teaspoons PK boost pH'd

Day 102-105

Gallon of water, 4 teaspoons Ionic Bloom nutrients, pH'd

Day 108-110:

Gallon of water, pH'd

Day 111: FLUSH

The flushing of your plant is very important. We flush these plants to get all the nutrients out of the soil and it will make your plant taste better and burn smoother. It also helps force all the remaining nutrients into the plant to help the yield.

For every gallon of soil (3-gallon pot has 3-gallon soil) you want to give your plant 3 gallons of water. For our 3-gallon pots we will flush with 9 gallons of water.

Place your plant in a bathtub or somewhere water can drain continuously. Slowly pour your first gallon of water into the pot.

YOU WILL NOT HURT YOUR PLANT.

You do not want the water overflowing out of the pot so slowly just let the water drain through the soil. Keep giving it gallon after gallon until you have giving it 9 gallons.

Day 112-126:

We will continue with every 2-3 days of water. Towards the end of your plants life it will drink the water much faster to make its yield bigger.

3 DAYS BEFORE CHOP DAY

You will give your last watering when you are 3 days away from chopping your plant. You will give a gallon of pH'd water. You want your dirt to be dry when it is time to chop. This will make chopping and drying much easier.

Chop Day:

Using your trimming scissors, cut off each branch and trim off all fan leaves. Anything that is sticking outside of the CBD flower that is a sugar leaf or stem can be cut off. Repeat this process for the whole plant. Tie string to each branch and hang upside down for 3-7 days.

We hang the branches inside our tent with lights off. You want your humidity around 45-55% for the whole 3-7 days. If it drops below 45 it will dry your buds out too much and affect your yield. If it raises above 60% there is a chance your flower will grow mold.

You will know the flower is ready because the stem will easily snap. If the stems only bend your flower is not ready yet. After branches can snap, cut the CBD enriched flower off branches and place in jars. Fill each jar with maximum amount of flower, forcing less air to be left inside of jar.

Burping Jars:

For the first two weeks of your freshly jarred CBD you will "burp your jars". You will burp jars twice a day. As soon as you wake up take the lid off jars for about 10 mins, then place back on. Before you go to bed, take off the lid of the jars for 10 mins, then replace again. This helps release excess moisture and inside of your flower and helps keep the flavor intact. After the two weeks of the twice daily, you can switch to once a day, for 5 mins for about another two weeks. Everyone has a preferred dryness or wetness to their CBD so everyone will have their own preference.

Curing:

After the burping of the jars you will now need to cure the CBD. The main reason for curing your flowers are to help with potency and flavor. The chemicals inside the flower break down over time, this helps take away from the earthy plant taste and smell leaving you with tasteful aromatic flowers. Leave your plants in your jars for as long as you'd like with lids on. You can sample your product at this point if you wanted to get an early sneak peek. I personally recommend a minimum of 1 month of curing. The longer they cure, the better they smell and taste. Feel free to open and smell the jars throughout the curing process.

Finish:

Now that your flower has had time to cure, it is ready to be used at its full potential. Enjoy the fresh, therapeutic aromas while handling your flower. (highly recommend taking a big whiff when you open the jar for the first time). You can burn the flower in joints, bongs, pipes, or bubblers. You may also decarboxylate the flower to use it for edibles. However, you use your fresh curated bud, enjoy every part of it!

Made in the USA
Las Vegas, NV
04 December 2023